, Boulto

How it is made

Motor Cars

Text   John Taylor
Design   Arthur Lockwood

Contents

ff

faber and faber in association with Threshold Books

All kinds of cars

Nowadays it is almost impossible to imagine a world without automobiles, yet it is only one hundred years since Karl Benz, in Germany, built the first production car. It had three wheels, and its speed was 15 kilometres per hour (9mph). At the same time, Gottlieb Daimler, also in Germany, was working on a four-wheeler powered by a single cylinder engine. Later, the two manufacturers were to combine, as Daimler-Benz, which is still one of the world's leading vehicle makers.

Exactly where and when the automobile actually had its origins is open to argument, though we know for sure that in Paris in 1770 Cugnot introduced his prototype for a steam-driven gun carriage. In the succeeding century there were many more experiments, particularly with steam, but it was the introduction of Otto's **internal combustion engine** in 1876 that enabled real progress to be made.

The first vehicles were very primitive, unreliable and uncomfortable, but in three decades they had begun to evolve into the motor cars that we know today – with **pneumatic**

Many examples of cars of the pioneer years have survived in museums and private hands, and are brought out for rallies and special occasions. This photograph was taken at the London to Brighton Veteran Car Run, which is held each November. Only cars built up to the end of 1904 are eligible.

tyres, multi-cylinder engines, electric starting and lighting, effective **suspension**, and attractive coachwork.

These custom-built models were very expensive to produce, and only the wealthy could afford to buy them, so manufacturers in Britain, Germany, France and the US looked around for ways in which they could speed up production. Inspiration came from the clockmakers, who were finding that with interchangeable parts they could produce clocks on a large scale. However, the real break-through came in 1909 in the United States, when Henry Ford set up organized production lines in his factory at Detroit, Michigan.

The function of a motor car is to carry people and their baggage on long or short journeys for business or for pleasure. It may be a saloon, a hatchback, an estate, or a coupé, and there are many variations of these four main categories. Sports cars and open cars are enjoying a revival. Everyday cars are 'customized', with polished wheels, hand-fitted panels and striking paintwork. Some car owners lovingly restore 'vintage' cars, enjoying their funny old ways and taking them to rallies where others can see and enjoy them.

Though most cars today are mass produced for a wide market there are still craftsmen companies who will either create or convert them for particular needs. A Head of State may want special coachwork. A businessman may want a

standard saloon cut, extended, lavishly trimmed and even armoured against possible terrorist attacks. Often these beautifully finished vehicles are produced in quite modest premises, by craftsmen skilled in the traditional ways.

However, such luxuries are for a very small minority, and most people have to be content with the standard, workmanlike saloons which play an indispensable part in their daily lives. In Britain, there are over 17 million cars and 25 million of the population hold driving licences, with almost a million passing the test every year. Cars are owned by 60 per cent of British households and 15 per cent of these own more than one. Of all the journeys made in Britain, 84 per cent are by private transport.

If we were still trying to use the horse as the prime means of movement on such a scale as we now know, life would quickly become impossible.

A vital factor in the progress of everyday motoring has been the development of Grand Prix racing and rally cars. Light alloys for engines, special metals for body construction, disc braking, and suspension technology have all been proven under the most arduous conditions on racetracks and rally circuits. One of the most important developments has been in tyre technology, where rubber compounds and construction methods have been adopted to meet the extreme demands of racing.

Looking behind the scenes in car manufacture reveals vast uses of resources, ever-rising levels of technology and increasing co-operation as well as competition on an intercontinental scale.

The customized car can take on any form that the owner asks for, as these two contrasting examples show. Above is a beach-buggy based on a Volkswagen Beetle, with glass-fibre body, oversize wheels and stylish paintwork. Below is the American Presidential limousine with its luxurious interior and special protective features such as bullet-proof glass.

The modern Grand Prix racing car, and the sports racing car (such as this Lancia), bear little resemblance to a day-to-day family car, but mechanically they have the same basis. The very high demands made on racing engines and other mechanical parts provide an excellent means of testing new materials for production cars.

The parts of a car

The modern car is made up of several thousand
items, ranging from large steel panels to very
small clips, all working together to provide a
comfortable ride for the occupants and space
for their luggage. This sectioned view of a Ford
Sierra shows how the major items fit beneath the
skin of the car.

1 The **engine** on this car is
mounted in-line with the
direction of travel, and drives
the rear wheels. Others are
mounted at right angles, and
drive the front wheels.

2 **Gearbox** This takes the
power from the engine and
transmits it through a set of
ratios or speeds to the wheels.

3 **Final drive.** Differential
gears turn the drive through
right angles to rotate the road
wheels.

4 **Road wheels and tyres.**
The tyres provide grip, and
act with the suspension to
give a comfortable ride.

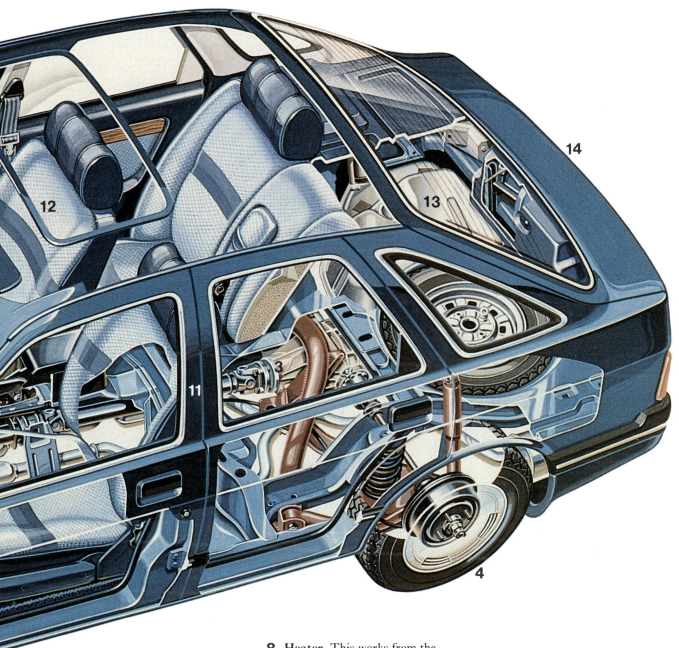

5 **Brakes.** Those on the front are disc brakes, those at the rear are drum brakes. They are operated by hydraulic pressure boosted by a servo pump driven by the engine.

6 **Suspension.** The suspension consists of springs and shock absorbers which are arranged to give a comfortable ride, as well as accurate handling on all road conditions.

7 **Radiator.** By a flow of air taken in at the front of the car the radiator cools the water which circulates around the engine.

8 **Heater.** This works from the engine cooling system. With hot water it heats air and blends it with cool air from outside to provide warmth for the driver and passengers.

9 The **floorpan** is the platform on which the car body is built up.

10 The **A pillar** on which the front doors are hung and which locates the windscreen is a major structural component of the body shell.

11 The **B pillar** supports the rear doors and the catches for the front doors. It is also a main post, giving the body its rigidity.

12 The **seats** are securely fixed to the floor by their steel frames and are trimmed with foam covered in cloth or vinyl facings, to provide comfort for the occupants.

13 The **rear boot** (trunk) houses the luggage and the spare wheel.

14 The **tailgate** lifts from roof level to provide easy access for loading.

15 The **steering wheel** is mounted on a jointed column designed to collapse in an accident, thus avoiding injury to the driver.

Designing the car

The design team at work producing sketches which will be the basis of the new model. Many hundreds of drawings are made, and the final design incorporates the best features.

From the design sketches and drawings a scale model is produced. Its features and dimensions are programmed into a computer for scaling up to the full-size car.

To determine accurately the interior dimensions and layout, a full-size plywood dummy is made. This enables the designers to adjust the layout in various ways to suit the body.

Before anyone puts pen to drawing board or – as is usually the case nowadays – fingers to computer keyboard, the manufacturer must have a clear idea of what he is going to build and for whom. The cost of a new model, to be produced in huge numbers and involving several factories (often in different countries) is so enormous that no car producer can afford to get it wrong. As the motor industry feeds a world more and more hungry for cars, the demands become more and more competitive, so that it is crucial to produce the right car for the right market.

The manufacturer must therefore make use of market research; of feedback from existing customers and buyers of competing cars; of the views of the dealers who sell the product and the correspondents of motoring newspapers and periodicals who test and comment on them. He can then evaluate what the desires and needs of the customer will be.

'Will be' are the key words, for the production of a new popular model from the drawing board to its arrival in the showroom can take up to five years. Often it is a case of 'leap-frogging', for as one car reaches production, plans are already being laid for its eventual successor.

Once the design specification has been drawn up, the first need is to decide just how much of the new model will actually be *new*. In fact, few cars are entirely new, for there is in the industry what is known as 'carry over' from existing models. The car may have an entirely new body, but the range of engines in differing sizes can include two units already used for other models,

Colour plays an important part in modern car design. The body paint has to be matched, or 'keyed', to the interior fabrics to provide a co-ordinated result. Here a colour stylist at Ford is comparing fabric and paint samples.

and a brand new or heavily updated design. Similarly, gearboxes can be from existing models or even bought in from another manufacturer. Brakes, wheels and other mechanical units can also be carried forward, and basic suspension designs can be adapted. In this way, production and development costs can be kept to a minimum, though many millions of pounds are still involved.

Body design stems from the stylist and his team, following the specifications laid down by the company. The styling team either work 'in-house', directly within the factory, or they may be a separate design company employed by many different manufacturers.

At this stage the drawing board plays a prominent part, as the designer must produce coloured sketches for initial approval. From this follows a full-size mock-up built in clay and

wood, and very cleverly finished with trim and paint to look like the real thing. Management and other interested people can thus see the car as it will eventually appear, and can express their opinions for or against.

After a decision on the final shape has been reached, and after the mechanical specification has been agreed, the latest modern technology is applied.

The 1980s have seen a revolution in automotive design techniques with the advent of **Computer Aided Design** (CAD). By using a computer, the designer dispenses with the drawing board and is able to take a new model and develop it to a very advanced stage without building even a single prototype. This results not only in considerable cost savings but also cuts down the time needed and brings the launch day of the new car much closer.

The **mainframe** computer builds up a data base from which engineers can work on individual aspects of design in complete harmony with each other. The clay model supplies much of the information in the form of **numerical co-ordinates**. The build-up of body and components on computers enables the engineer to determine the right section of metal for its task: not too heavy, nor too light, thus achieving the ideal balance between weight and strength. With the computer the engineer can 'test' the component, to evaluate its strength. He can also see how it will behave in actual use, even to the point of crash testing on the **Visual Display Unit** (VDU) screen – for he knows that the completed prototype will behave in a similar way in actual physical tests.

The resulting data are finally compiled and translated into vehicle production.

To produce an accurate impression of how the finished car will look, the styling studio builds a full-size mock-up in wood and clay, complete with paint and trim. Exact dimensions are provided by the computer.

Building in safety

All car design is a matter of compromise. The sleek shape has to be matched with the ability to carry passengers in comfort. The largest possible internal space has to be provided, with the most compact external dimensions. Performance must be lively, but economy is even more vital. Entry and general access must be as easy as possible for driver and passengers, but the body structure of the car must be very rigid.

The computer can reach the ideal solutions to the problems, but safety still involves physical testing and the ability to meet a multitude of national and international regulations.

For reasons such as these, manufacturers spend vast sums of money providing their own research and development centres as well as using others which are internationally recognized. The centres tackle everything likely to be associated with the car in the foreseeable future as well as factors already associated with it. They can range from the evaluation of new materials for components, to wind tunnel testing of complete vehicles. In between are found the computers, design studios, automatic drawing machines and even pilot production facilities with robot assembly.

The safety factor involves virtually every feature of the car. The basic design is tested on tracks with special types of surface conditions intended to show up any deficiencies in the steering and roadholding. Braking receives similar attention; the advance of anti-lock braking systems with their ability to maintain steering accuracy on wet and icy surfaces is now making them practical and economic for cheaper mass-produced cars.

Computers can predict how bodywork behaves in an accident – but testing is a compulsory requirement for what is known as 'type approval', the granting of which enables a car to be sold in production quantities. The body must not only provide a strong **cell** to protect the occupants; it must deform correctly, with bonnet and boot absorbing shocks by crumpling in a predetermined manner. The engine must be deflected beneath the car in a frontal collision rather than into the driving compartment. The fuel tank must be mounted where it is most protected from damage, usually low down and ahead of the rear axle. The passenger doors must not burst open in a crash and must contribute to the complete body strength.

Inside the car, the designers must avoid sharp edges and projections, providing soft **trim** which will either absorb impact shock or break off under a specified loading likely to occur if an occupant hits it in an accident. Seats must be properly fixed to the floor. Belt systems must be mounted for safety, comfort and convenience.

Mercedes-Benz now offers an air bag restraint system mounted in the boss of the steering wheel. In a crash the bag is inflated by a gas cylinder to provide a deep pillow which protects the driver's face from the steering wheel. The bag quickly deflates to leave the seat belt holding the passenger safely.

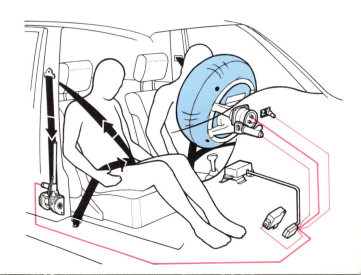

Crash testing is a vital part of all car development. This sequence of pictures shows a Nissan Bluebird hitting a concrete block at 50kph (30mph). The damage is confined to the engine compartment, and the passenger area is undamaged.

Smooth air flow, shown here being checked with smoke trails in a wind tunnel, ensures an efficient body shape and low wind noise levels.

The **flammability** of materials used must also be considered. No car is fireproof, but care in the choice of fabrics and plastics can minimize the potentially lethal fumes given off in a fire. Comfort and ergonomics – the science of placing controls in the most convenient positions in relation to the driver – also come under the safety heading. If the driver is uncomfortable in his seat, it can affect his performance. Similarly, high noise levels can prove tiring and possibly harmful. The climate also plays its part, for if the car is poorly ventilated or if the temperature is hard to control, the driver's reactions can be slowed. This is one reason why manufacturers test cars in the extremes of world temperature, from the Arctic to the deserts, as well as reproducing these conditions in the laboratory.

Regulations have governed the motor car from its beginnings, when a man with a red flag walked in front to warn the public that a horseless carriage was approaching. Almost every country has its own set of motoring rules, ranging from basics such as speed limits and driving on the right or left, to advanced stipulations on noise levels and exhaust emissions.

In general, regulations are designed to protect the occupants of the car, the public in general, and the environment around them. In some cases they can have a more political implication, aimed at protecting the commercial interests of the country concerned. However, whether he likes them or not, every car manufacturer must meet the regulations of each country in which he wishes to sell his products. As well as being lengthy and laborious, the process of obtaining approval can also involve expensive testing. All of these factors have to be reflected in the eventual price of the car.

Fire is a hazard in a car, and the petrol tank is the most dangerous part. Here a tank is being tested in a laboratory.

Cars must be made to work in every possible temperature. As well as carrying out tests in different parts of the world, technicians create conditions artificially in a laboratory. In recent years, batteries, lubricants and heaters have all been greatly improved.

How a car is built

Building the modern car on a moving production line involves constructing the body piece by piece and then incorporating the mechanical and other components which have been made elsewhere.

The typical assembly line shown here starts with sheet metal fed to the press shop, where a series of giant stamping machines cuts out the individual pieces of metal which will make up the body. In most cases the pieces are formed and trimmed into their final shapes in one operation.

From here the parts of the underbody, or **floorpan** are first welded together on the moving line, to be joined by the front structure, sides, roof, wings, bonnet, doors and tailgate/bootlid. Now formed into a complete shell, the car body moves through the complex painting process. Then comes the fitting of the windows, dashboard, trim and seats. The mechanical units are fitted last. Finally comes the testing, cleaning and signing-off for delivery.

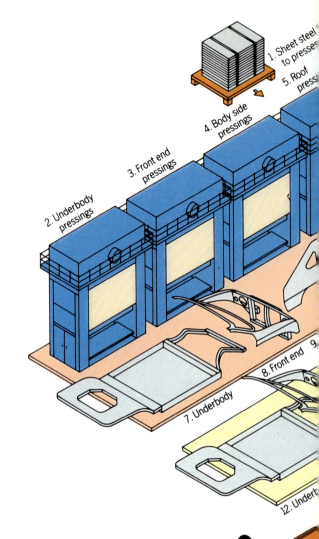

1. Sheet steel to presses
2. Underbody pressings
3. Front end pressings
4. Body side pressings
5. Roof press
7. Underbody
8. Front end
9.
12. Underb

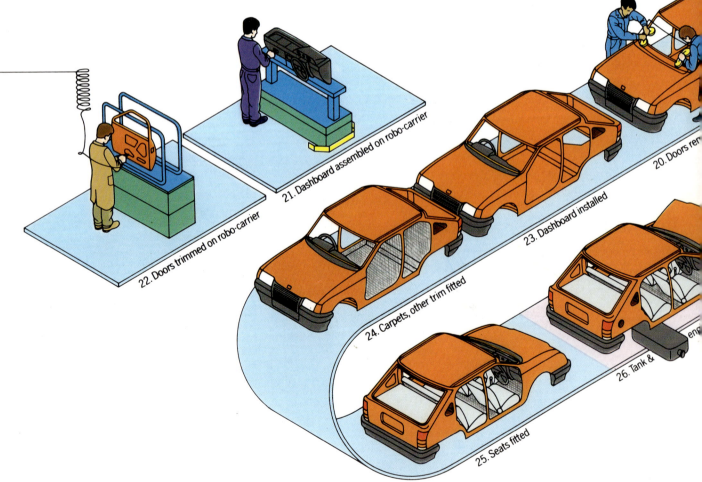

20. Doors rem
21. Dashboard assembled on robo-carrier
22. Doors trimmed on robo-carrier
23. Dashboard installed
24. Carpets, other trim fitted
25. Seats fitted
26. Tank &

10. Roof   11. Door

14. Roof added

13. Body sides added

15. Doors, bonnet, wings & tailgate added

16. Body protection and base primer dip

17. Spray primer

...joined

18. Spray paint

19. Under wing waxing

29. Doors re-fitted

28. Petrol in

30. Roller tests

27. Wheels on

31. Body wash

32. Conditioning and valeting

34. Brakes tested

33. Engine and underbody waxed

35. Quality control sign off

36. Drive-away

11

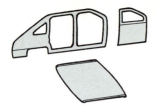

Pressing panels

The many pieces which together make up a complete car body share a common origin. They all start life as sheets of steel that come to the car plant from the mill either in giant rolls like newsprint, or as rectangular sheets in bales.

To transform these into components involves two main operations: cutting and shaping. Both are carried out on a series of huge **presses**, some as high as a house and together filling a workshop as large in area as up to three soccer pitches. The presses are of different sizes according to their actual task, the biggest having a capacity of up to 1500 tonnes.

The sheet steel is first cut on automatic guillotines ready for feeding to the presses. These take the components through stages of production according to their individual complexity. A simple panel such as a complete side can often be stamped and formed in one operation, whereas pillars need shaping several times.

Recently, automation has come to the fore in the press shop as well as in other areas of the factory. Overhead cranes move the raw material. On the presses, feeding and removal is controlled automatically. The dies on which the actual forming is carried out are of high-precision steel and can be removed rapidly for regular cleaning or replacement.

On modern assembly lines where more than one model of car is handled at a time, control of the output and supply of components is by computer.

When the panels are pressed from the sheets, large quantities of waste metal are left over. This has to be removed to underground **hoppers** where conveyors take it outside for baling. It is then returned to the steel mill for reprocessing.

Until recently the cutting and shaping of metal on such a huge scale was an extremely noisy operation. Nowadays the noisy areas are enclosed as much as possible, and sound is reduced to the minimum. Press shops were once gloomy places, but in recent times great improvements have taken place, and in the best factories they are now as light, airy and colourful as possible. A pleasant working environment is very important, for though automation takes care of many processes, skilled workers still have to oversee the various operations and to clean and change the dies.

At this stage of production, completed panels and other components can easily be damaged if they are not handled properly after pressing. Items coming off the presses are therefore housed in racks with protective surfaces to ensure that every component reaches the assembly line in perfect condition.

CAD/CAM (Computer Aided Design/Computer Aided Manufacture) plays a major part in the creation of the modern car. Here technicians check aspects of design on the visual display screen.

Steel comes from the mills in giant rolls (as seen here) or in baled sheets. The rolls are cut into sheets before being fed to the presses.

A modern press shop, showing doors being produced for the Ford Escort. Each component is built up in a series of presses, and completed items are loaded into trucks to be taken to the assembly line by the tractor (which can be seen between the presses).

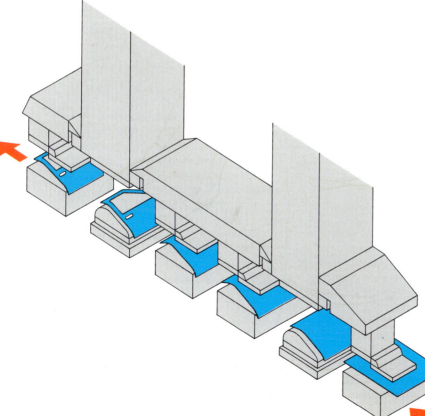

A typical forming sequence in a press shop. Here a door is built up, starting on the right with the steel sheet, through forming and cutting to shape, to provide the completed panel.

Making the underbody

The underbody, or floorpan as it is also known, is the most complex part of the car's body. Its design must be shaped to allow for the wheel arches, the well of the boot with the spare wheel housing, the exhaust system, and in the case of a rear wheel drive car the transmission tunnel. All these features have to be fitted snugly within the shape of the floorpan, which must also form a rigid base for the sides and roof of the body.

Partly because of its size, but also because it can be varied for different models, the floorpan is made up of a number of pressings. In this way some of it can be used for saloon, hatchback and estate, and in shortened wheelbase form it can also allow for a coupé body.

If you were to look down on a complete underbody you would see a shape which has wells for the seating, inlets to take the wheel arches and a sink-like hollow into which the spare wheel fits. The front looks like two arms extending to cradle the engine and front suspension. Even on a car which is driven by the front wheels there is still a central hump where the exhaust and brake cables fit; this also adds considerably to the rigidity of the structure.

The first part of the body to be assembled is the **underframe**, and this is where production on the assembly line begins. It is also the first point at which robots are encountered. The use of computer-controlled robots for welding the sections together not only assures greater accuracy: it also avoids the boring repetitive manual welding that used to be a feature of car construction. The computer and the robot have now taken over much of the monotonous work in car building which once had to be carried out manually.

The different pressings which combine to form the underbody come together on the assembly line direct from the press shop. Again, they are supplied in the right quantity at the right place with the help of a computer.

The pressings fit on to jigs on the assembly line. These are specially shaped cradles which hold each item accurately in place while they are welded together.

Not so long ago the completed underbody had to be pushed by hand along the line to the next work station. Today it is moved automatically – sometimes by overhead conveyor – to the point at which the body begins to take on its recognizable shape.

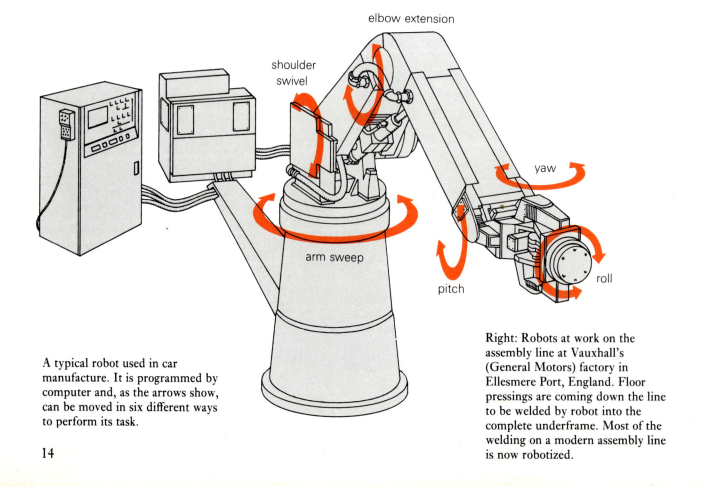

A typical robot used in car manufacture. It is programmed by computer and, as the arrows show, can be moved in six different ways to perform its task.

Right: Robots at work on the assembly line at Vauxhall's (General Motors) factory in Ellesmere Port, England. Floor pressings are coming down the line to be welded by robot into the complete underframe. Most of the welding on a modern assembly line is now robotized.

Building the body

With the arrival of the underfloor at the next work station the 'carousel' is brought into use. This is a large jig which positions the body-sides with perfect accuracy, so that they are ready to be welded automatically to the underbody, again by robot.

As each new car model is introduced, more and more of the welding is carried out by robots. On a modern car there are around 2,500 spot welds: the single welds which hold various parts together. (The continuous joint known as seam welding has largely been discontinued.) Up to 90 per cent of the spot welds are applied by robots,

Welding a body side for the Rover 800. The pieces are clamped accurately together in a jig and welded automatically.

When the side section is completed it is removed by overhead conveyor to the next assembly stage, where it will join the other body components.

every one of them in exactly the same position on each body. In modern body assembly up to 130 robots are employed, avoiding much heavy work by hand. These robots have a built-in 'memory' which enables them to cater for different body types – such as saloon and hatchback – which may be on their way along the assembly line.

In the same way, the roof is positioned and welded in place, while the doors are built on nearby assembly lines. Making a car door is a task involving several different pressings, the outer **skin** being clinched over its inner frame by a process known as hemming, before the pressings are welded together. It is usual for doors to be fitted to a car in the early stages of assembly then removed after painting, to allow for final interior completion before they are fitted to the same body.

Once the frame is complete it must be checked for accuracy. Many items are 'random-checked' – that is, one of a batch of bodies is taken off the line and placed in a special jig where it can be measured accurately against the original specification.

A technique now coming into increasing use involves the application of the **industrial laser**. By this method every car body, on completion, can be measured at a separate work station where laser beams are projected from many different angles. The beams show up the slightest degree of distortion in any body. With modern construction methods, body structures are generally very accurate, but checking by laser provides accurate quality control which is vitally important to the completed car. Should for any reason a body be out of alignment, it can well affect the handling of the finished car, in the same way as an uneven foundation can cause distortion in a whole house.

Watching a car body going along the production line in a modern factory you can sometimes see a small metal cylinder hanging underneath. This is an electronic device housing a **transponder**. Each transponder is programmed with information relating to that particular body, telling the assembly robots and other machinery that it is, say, a five-door hatchback. In this way it is built automatically, and different body styles can come along the line in random patterns according to production requirements.

Welding body frames on the assembly line. The use of automated jigs and clamps to hold the sections together, and robots to weld them, ensures complete accuracy every time.

Industrial lasers are now being used by manufacturers such as the Rover Group to carry out precise checks on a bodyshell's dimensions after assembly. This saves considerable time compared with former manual measuring processes, as well as being more accurate.

Mounting a transponder on a car body in the initial stages of assembly. This electronic device is pre-programmed to identify the body as it goes through the manufacturing process. It contains information on the model, trim and finish.

Painting and body sealing

The primer, or base coat of paint, is applied to the car body shell by immersion in a bath which holds thousands of gallons of paint. The body is taken through the bath suspended from an overhead conveyor. The cable seen in the foreground is an electrical contact, and thus energized the body shell attracts a smooth and even coating to all surfaces.

Heat is an important part of the painting process. The painted body goes through high temperature ovens which not only dry the paint but bake it on to the body to provide a lasting and durable finish.

The painting of a car body ensures that it is protected for life, as well as providing it with a colourful finish. The cost of this process is very high, running into millions of pounds.

Once the body is assembled, it must be thoroughly cleaned before it can be painted. Thus the first stage in its long journey by overhead conveyor is through a de-greasing tank. It is then rinsed off.

The first of up to six or even seven coatings to be applied is a phosphate, which makes the body receptive to paint. Before the painting processs can begin, the body is examined under strong lights to ensure that there are no blemishes, and it then enters the paint shop. The bumpers – to be painted in the same colour – are slung underneath.

More rinsing follows, the final rinse being with **demineralized water** so that the surface will be blemish-free and able to take the paint without it flaking off. The next stage is the drying. Then the base primer coatings are applied layer by layer, the body either being totally immersed or sprayed for each coat. Two further coats of primer follow, one of them applied to areas where the body needs particular protection against chipping from stones. These coats are sprayed **electrostatically**, using an electrical field in which the body is connected to electrodes and the paint is drawn on to complete the electrical field.

The final layers of paint are an **acrylic** sealer and the acrylic top-coat. With some metallic finishes, a clear lacquer coat is applied over the

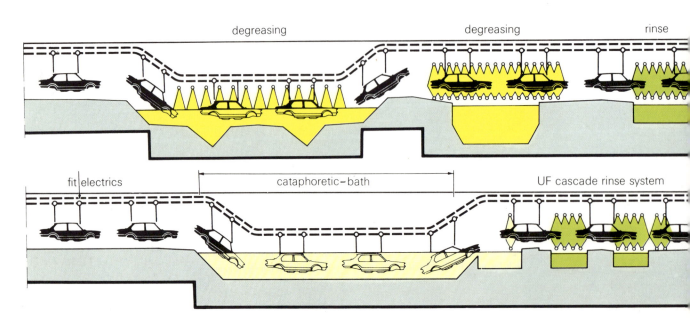

degreasing   degreasing   rinse

fit electrics   cataphoretic–bath   UF cascade rinse system

acrylic. To protect the body against rust, the steel pressings used for the vulnerable lower areas exposed to road salt are made up of zinc-coated steel which has a specially high resistance to corrosion.

Special wax is injected into hollow body sections such as **pillars** and **sills**, to keep moisture out. The underside is also treated with a polythene coating to increase resistance further. A bitumen-based flexible coating is applied to the underside to provide a coat against water, snow, grit, stones and salt. Methods such as these have enabled manufacturers to offer guarantees against corrosion for periods of six years or more. In the past, the body often rusted away, while the engine and other mechanical units were still good for many years.

Automatic spraying of the top coat of paint to the car body. In many factories, inaccessible areas of the body are still painted by hand-held spray guns, though robots are steadily taking over.

Injecting a special mixture of wax and oil into holes built into the body sections. This gives an even coating to protect the metal against corrosion.

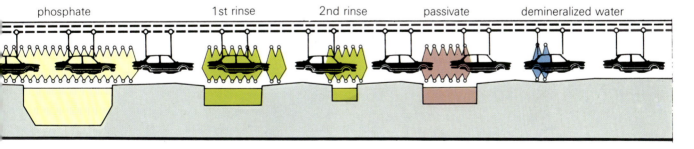

phosphate   1st rinse   2nd rinse   passivate   demineralized water

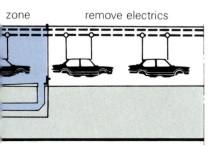

zone   remove electrics

Pretreating and finishing the body shell is a long process involving several stages. This diagram shows the pretreatment section at the Lancia factory in Turin, Italy. On the left, the body enters and goes through successive degreasing, rinsing, phosphating, washing, prime coating and drying stages.

Components from many places

A manufacturer's own design studios produce a choice of full-size models of components, such as the steering wheels seen here. Once the final design is selected, the go-ahead is given for production either within the company or by a specialist supplier.

These days to refer to a car as 'Made in Britain', 'Made in the United States' or 'Made in Germany' is rather misleading. What is usually meant by, say, 'Made in Britain', is 'Assembled in Britain', for the many components that go to make up the modern car have often come from many different factories in several countries.

To take an example: a typical product of one of the giant multi-nationals such as Ford or General Motors, whose headquarters are in the United States, can be assembled in Spain, which has developed a large capacity for car assembly in recent years. The sheet steel for the body pressings will have come from Britain, Germany or even Spain itself. The engine has been produced in a factory in South Wales, its sparking plugs and electrical components have come from Northern Ireland, and its fuel injection equipment from Germany. The brakes are British (from the Midlands) and so are the headlights and windscreen wiper motors; the wiper blades and arms have been made in West London. The rack and pinion steering gear is also British and the suspension units are from Germany. Wheels are British, but the tyres are French (Michelin), Italian (Pirelli), British (Dunlop, Goodyear) or from other sources. In the case of one popular estate car, some pressings and items even come from Australia, where the model originated.

As far as the **transmission** is concerned, the gearbox could be from a German factory or, in the case of an automatic, from France.

Engine assembly. Although the process is highly automated on a moving track, skilled assembly fitters still play a vital part.

Right: Making tyres is a combination of automation and highly-skilled hand work. In the foreground of this picture an Avon radial-ply car tyre is seen in its uncured form, ready to go into the moulding press. The operator is removing a finished tyre at the end of the curing line.

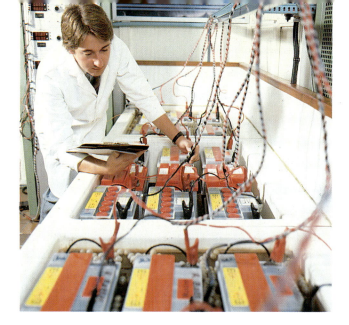

All components, whether supplied from a company outside or a factory within the car maker's own empire, are subjected to continual testing programmes to ensure that they meet the specifications laid down. Here, a Ford engineer tests car batteries.

For the 'finish', the paint also comes from Germany, the seats, carpets, trim panels and the dashboard from Britain, and the radio from Holland, Germany or Japan.

The actual origin of components can vary, and even the same model of a car can be built in different countries. For instance, in the case of Ford, some Escorts are built at Halewood in Liverpool, but the high performance models come from Cologne. Again, with Vauxhall (General Motors), the Cavalier is built at Luton, at the sister Opel factory in Russelsheim am Main in Germany, or Antwerp in Belgium. In this way, the manufacturer retains a high degree of flexibility, being able to balance the flow between countries where necessary, and to phase out a model from one factory in order to introduce a successor.

The major manufacturers produce many components themselves. Steering, fuel pumps, electrical items, radiators, wheels, seat belts, hoses and piping can all come from different factories within the organization.

When it comes to outside suppliers – the specialist component makers who provide other essential items – the big car manufacturers often adopt what is known as a 'dual sourcing' policy. This means that two or possibly more firms will be making identical units for a particular model of car at any given time. The reason for this is that it enables pricing to be competitive. It also lessens the possibility of a hold-up should one supplier be unable to meet schedules due to, say, an industrial dispute or a factory fire. With a car, the old adage of 'for the want of a nail, the horseshoe was lost' is very real, for vehicles coming from the factory at the rate of a thousand or more a day, complete in every way except for one vital item, are an embarrassment and create a vast storage problem.

Bringing the right components together in the right quantities at the right time demands meticulous planning, and today, once again, the computer plays a vital rôle. The car-maker tends to keep as little material on the assembly site as possible, and he depends on the outside factories to keep the parts coming in the correct quantities. This is known as the **KanBan system** (Japanese for 'just in time') and saves a large amount of expensive factory space as well as the cost of lighting, heating and general maintenance.

While much of the material is carried from factory to factory by shuttles of heavy trucks, rail also plays an important part, especially where international movement is concerned. Modern factories are usually planned with their own rail links right into the assembly building, with siding capacity to handle large freight trains. Of course, where the movement is intercontinental, much goes by sea in the same way as the finished product. Huge freighters travel around the world, specially built as vast garages which the cars are driven into in one country and driven out in another country thousands of miles away, at a dockside receiving centre. Then they go back again with components and raw materials.

The use of automated machinery, robots and driverless electric tractors delivering components to moving assembly lines demands careful control. This supervisor at the General Motors Vauxhall factory at Ellesmere Port keeps control of the system with the aid of television screens, visual computer displays and direct telephone contact.

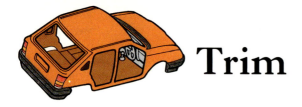

Trim

Now that the body is complete, though temporarily without its doors, the next process is fitting out the interior on its journey through the factory.

Here the car becomes more than a skeleton, for its 'nerves' are now installed. These are the electrical wires without which the car would be useless. The wiring is built up on boards from reels of different coloured wires for simple identification. The result is a complete wiring harness rather like a garden plant, with the wires bound together as a main stem, spreading with roots at one end and branches at the other, leading from the engine compartment to the instruments, and so on.

After the harness has been installed, the dashboard is put in place. This is a complete unit, moulded in plastic, with the instruments and switches ready for connecting up. At this stage, either before or during installation, the instrumentation is tested to check that gauges and lights are working properly. The steering wheel is bolted to the bulkhead, ready for connecting to the steering gear.

Before the carpets are fitted, the underfelt must be laid down. This adds to passenger comfort underfoot but, more important, it is also sound-deadening. During body assembly, sound-deadening materials have been fixed in areas where drumming or vibration could be a source of discomfort to the occupants. The underfelt adds to this insulation. The floor carpets are moulded into shape so that they fit snugly all round.

Next the seats are fitted into place, having been built in the factory or supplied by a specialist maker. Here again, control is important, as the more luxurious the car, the better must be the seats, while all the interior is colour-keyed to the paintwork. This means that the upholstery,

Working conditions on modern assembly lines are designed to be as fatigue-free as possible. Not only are they convenient for the worker but they also ensure a higher standard of work. Here the steering system is being fitted to a Mercedes-Benz 190 at their factory in Bremen, Germany. The car is held in a rotating frame so that all areas are readily accessible.

Compared with other areas of car manufacture the trim shop has changed little in its essentials. Seats and carpets are still machined by skilled workers, though now on a vast scale in order to meet modern production demands. This is the trim shop in a Ford factory.

Right: Even completed seats are now put into place by robot in some factories. In this Japanese Nissan line the doors have been removed to provide complete access to the interior.

carpet and door trim must be in the correct shade. Once more, the computer plays a vital role in seeing that all goes smoothly. The other main item of interior trim is the roof lining, which is made up in one piece so that it can be fitted through the front or rear windscreen aperture.

Once all this has been done, it is time to fix the front and rear windscreens. For many years, glass was held in place by means of a rubber glazing strip specially moulded to slot into the opening and to take the glass securely. Now, however,

more and more cars rely on bonded glazing, where the glass is actually stuck in place with special adhesives. This gives a smoother fit and reduces wind resistance and noise, while it also contributes to the overall rigidity of the body.

Robots are becoming common for carrying the glass and fitting it into place, thus avoiding laborious manual work and providing an exact fit.

While these other processes have been taking place, the doors have received their glass, locks and trim, and are ready to rejoin the body.

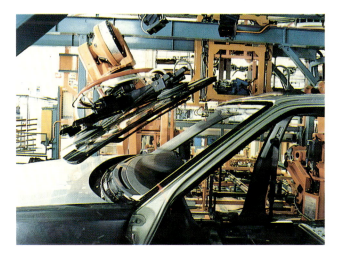

More and more new cars have bonded windscreens, heat sealed to the body instead of being fixed by rubber channels. On the Rover Group lines, for example, the windscreen is brought up and fixed by robot.

Right: Many factories use automatic robo-carriers to move components from one work station to another. These are guided by electric cables buried in the factory floor. Here, doors can be seen on the move.

Final assembly

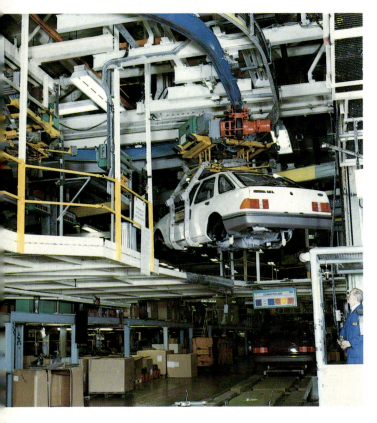

Overhead conveyors are used a great deal to move cars from one assembly stage to another, and often from one floor level or building to another. Here a Ford Sierra body moves to its next station at the Ford factory at Dagenham.

Fitting wheels is still carried out by hand, but the mechanic's task is made easier and quicker by the use of a power tool which fixes all four wheel nuts simultaneously.

The car is now like a skeleton covered with skin but awaiting heart, lungs, brain and muscles to make it complete. The heart is the engine; the lungs the fuel and carburation system; the brain the electronic controls; the muscles the transmission and final drive.

The correct mix of components for the particular model is brought together by the computer, aided by the faithful transponder which has accompanied the body throughout its construction.

The body now takes to the air on a conveyor line which raises it high enough to allow the assembly team to work comfortably. The engine is brought into position on a trolley with a built-in jacking system. This lifts it to fit into the engine compartment complete with clutch and gearbox ready for bolting into place. The piping and cables for fuel and electrical power are then connected.

Simultaneously, at the other end of the car, the fuel tank is mounted. This is generally just ahead of the rear axle, below the floor, where it is well protected from accident damage. Front and rear suspension follow, to be bolted into place. The steering is then connected to the steering wheel which has been fitted earlier. This method of assembly is specially designed to suit modern steering systems. The old-fashioned one-piece steering column has now been superseded by a jointed type which takes up less space and absorbs collision shock instead of acting like a long spear aimed directly at the driver.

After the radiator, battery, electronic controls and ancillary items have been fitted into place, the car is then lowered almost to floor level to receive its wheels and tyres. The wheel nuts are spun into place, a complete set at a time, with the aid of an hydraulic tool suspended on a cable and counterbalanced so that it can easily be manoeuvred into position by the operator.

The car is complete and ready for its life blood. Water and anti-freeze flow into the cooling system, the engine is filled with oil, the running gear is greased, and the tank is filled with petrol.

Now the car is in every detail ready for the road, but it cannot leave with a 'clean bill of health' until it has been thoroughly checked and tested to the satisfaction of the team of specialists who stand between it and the factory doors.

Mechanical units are built up on a separate line to be fed to the main line at the correct point. In this photograph, front suspension and steering units are being completed at a Ford factory.

A Ford Fiesta body joins forces with its mechanical components. The assembled steering and suspension is ready in position on a power operated platform which will raise it for bolting to the body.

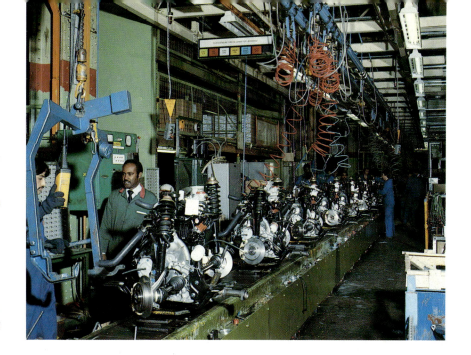

Finishing and testing

On its journey through the factory the car has been subjected at each stage of construction to a variety of separate tests. It must now undergo a complete test cycle designed to ensure that it is fully roadworthy and that it meets the specification. And there is still yet another test. On arrival at the dealer's premises it is given a pre-delivery inspection (PDI) before being handed over to the customer.

One of the most spectacular tests is the check for leaks. This is usually carried out by subjecting the car to a continuous high-pressure water spray, directed from various angles and equal to a very heavy rainstorm. Some highly advanced manufacturers employ what is known as a 'sniffing robot' which detects leaks without using water. The car is injected with a low-pressure mixture of air and helium, and robots which are programmed to cover all the joints and openings such as windows and doors, track over the body with sensors which detect any leak of the mixture.

The electrical system if not properly connected and checked could be a source of headaches, so car makers use a variety of testing systems with plug-in devices. The Rover Group has what is known as its Vehicle Electrical Test System (VETS) in which a computer identifies possible electrical faults with the aid of a probe which gives a read-out against the computerized test system. As a car can have up to 60 electrical circuits, this technique covers a complex programme in the shortest time with a high degree of efficiency.

For the last stage the dynamometer takes over. This device is a rolling road, or set of rollers, on which the car is run through a performance cycle to check that engine power is up to specification, while the 'driver' checks the gear change and pedal action. Headlights are also tested for correct height-setting and operation.

Some manufacturers prefer to put their cars through a real road test before giving them the go-ahead. The most efficient have private test tracks around their factories where finished cars all undergo a strict and demanding run over a variety of surfaces, gradients and angles designed to show up any faults in handling and performance.

Every car maker has, after the final checking area, what is known as a rectification bay, where cars which show any faults can be pulled off the line and cured of their ills. Even at this late stage it is normal to take a number of cars out of the line on each production shift so that further quality checks can be made.

Finally, polishing and valeting sees the car ready for signing-off and fit for delivery to the dealer.

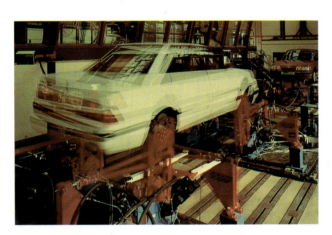

Tests and checks are made right through the manufacturing process. Here a Rover 800 is being put through a harsh vibration test to ensure that assembly is up to standard.

Right: International regulations concerning pollution and exhaust emission levels are becoming much more strict. Because of this, car manufacturers monitor their products very closely to ensure that requirements are met. This photograph shows a Ford Granada undergoing emission tests.

Top-quality production cars such as the Mercedes-Benz are built in the same way as other mass-market models, but there is considerable difference in the quality of materials, the actual design and the meticulous inspection standards. Mercedes S-class saloons are seen here at the end of the assembly line at their Stuttgart factory in Germany.

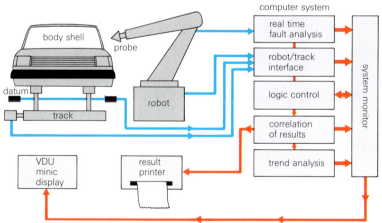

Testing for leaks in a car is usually carried out by spraying water on all the relevant parts. The Rover Group uses a robot to 'sniff' for leaks. A low pressure air and helium mixture is injected into the closed body, and the robot tracks over the body-seals, probing for leaks.

On completion, a road test on a specially-built track will pinpoint any faults in assembly.

Coachbuilding and customizing

Before press shops were introduced, car bodies were built up by hand, using rollers such as this, operated by a skilled worker with an experienced eye. Such work is still carried out today by specialist coachbuilders. Here a wing panel is seen being formed from sheet aluminium in the AC Cars factory.

The customer buying a hand-built car such as Rolls-Royce expects the best, and it is the maker's job to provide it. For example, the polished walnut veneers used for the interior trim have to be carefully selected and perfectly matched.

For most car owners the traditional skills of the carriage builder are associated only with the days of horse-drawn vehicles. Yet for those who want the very top model in the range, the smell of leather upholstery and the shine of wood veneer trim still prove irresistible.

Happily, there are still craftsmen with the skills needed to produce hand-built luxury cars. It is true that the Rolls-Royce of today generally has a steel body built like that of any other car, but there is still scope for the craftsmanship that has been synonymous with the name Rolls-Royce since the first decade of this century. The famous **radiator shell** is still built up by hand, using nickel silver-plated metal, soldered together with infinite care and with an eye for perfection. The famous bonnet mascot of the Rolls-Royce, known as the 'Spirit of Ecstasy', was designed in the company's early days by Charles Sykes. It is still made in the same way, cast by the **lost wax process** and hand-finished and polished before being plated.

Other cars compete with the Rolls-Royce and its sumptuous interior luxury, with polished walnut veneer for the fascia and door cappings, top quality Connolly hide for the supple leather seating and door panels, and deep Wilton carpet for the floor.

The Aston Martin is an example of a top-quality sporting car still built with a hand-made body. The immensely strong steel frame is panelled in aluminium sheeting, shaped on rollers by the skilled hands and experienced eye of a craftsman. Each panel has to be a perfect fit, and free from blemish even though it is to be hidden beneath many coats of paint. Aston Martin production is a long way removed from the computer and robot world of the mass production builder. At the company's factory at Newport

The method of casting the Rolls-Royce bonnet mascot was discovered by the Chinese about 4,000 years ago. It is known as the lost wax process.
1 A wax pattern is made.
2 It is covered by a heat-resistant material. The wax is melted away.
3 Casting metal is poured into the hole.
4 After cooling, the heat-resistant covering is chipped away, leaving a perfect reproduction of the pattern.

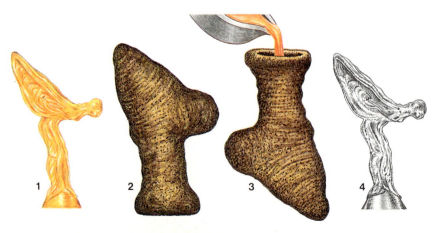

Pagnell in Buckinghamshire each of the famous V8 aluminium alloy engines is built up painstakingly by one skilled operator who works alone and who proudly mounts a plaque bearing his name on the completed engine.

Though the craft of the wheelwright has disappeared, many of the trades once familiar in the carriage era are still maintained, producing the highest quality cars for the most discerning customers, or 'clients' as they are usually called.

In a different way, many owners of everyday cars wish to stamp their individuality on their particular model, even if they cannot aspire to a Rolls-Royce or an Aston Martin. This is a market which has grown very rapidly in recent years and centres on the customizing trade. As well as ordering special tuning for engines, and modified suspension, the owner can also have the appearance of his saloon or hatchback altered to give it a sporty look. This is achieved by fitting mouldings in glass-fibre and other plastics as front or rear **spoilers** and side sills, to give the car a lower look. Special paint finishes, coloured stripes, and distinctive wheels complete the transformation. To the interior all sorts of equipment or trim can be added, including polished wood to give it a distinctive touch.

Between these two extremes lies another specialist service where the craftsman joins forces with the engineer to change the car's character.

This is provided by the coachbuilder who adapts a standard product to meet the demands of a certain sector of the car-buying market. Specialist coachbuilders can take a saloon, literally saw it in half, and fit a new centre section which will provide more space in the back; thus a saloon can be converted into a limousine for government or business use. The same coachbuilder might also build a hearse on a standard saloon, and this matches the lengthened luxury car in a chauffeur hire fleet. As well as skilfully cutting and 'stretching' the body, craftsmen work on the interior, trimming the wood, leather and carpet to the highest standards.

Several companies in Europe and the United States specialize in this work, which entails considerable strengthening of the body to ensure its rigidity. Other coachbuilders have created very stylish convertibles from standard production cars as different as Minis and Ford Capris. With the increasing popularity of open-air motoring, the big manufacturers either find a specialist to develop a convertible which they then build themselves, or they commission a coachbuilder to do it for them. In the world of the craftsman coachbuilder almost anything is possible, including six-wheel convertible Range Rovers.

Wherever there is a demand for something different, there is always a band of skilled and dedicated craftsmen ready to meet the challenge.

To lengthen a car, it must first be cut in half. Here specialist coachbuilders have sliced through a Ford Granada in order to turn it into a limousine. The design work is carried out in close co-operation with Ford.

The finished Grosvenor six-door limousine is not only longer than the original Granada. It is luxuriously finished inside with leather, deep carpets and polished wood veneers. The hatchback tailgate has been replaced by a standard lidded luggage boot.

Key dates

1886 Karl Benz introduced the world's first production car in Mannheim, Germany.
1890 Gottlieb Daimler began production of belt-driven cars (the forerunners of the Mercedes), at Stuttgart in Germany.
1894 The Duryea brothers built the USA's first car (which they called the Duryea).
1895 The first pneumatic tyres were used, in France, on a racing Peugeot.
1896 The Daimler Company of Coventry began operations, as the first British motor manufacturer.
1905 The first friction brake linings were introduced in England by Henry Frood, under the name Ferodo.
1909 Henry Ford set up the world's first car production line at Detroit, Michigan.
1912 The first car electric lighting and starting were introduced by Cadillac of Detroit.
1914 In the US, Dodge pioneered the modern pressed steel car body.
1916 The world's first mechanical windscreen wipers were introduced in the United States, some of them on Willys-Knight cars in Toledo, Ohio.
1919 Hispano-Suiza of Bois-Colombes in France introduced servo-assisted four-wheel brakes.
1920 Rolls-Royce began car production, in Springfield, Massachussetts, USA, which was to remain in operation until 1931.
1921 Hydraulic four-wheel brakes were introduced at Duesenberg in the US.
1922 Ford of America became the first company to build over one million cars in a year.
1924/5 Cellulose paints were introduced on the Oakland (General Motors) in the US, and the AC in England.
1926 Safety glass was introduced, in the US, by Studebaker.
1926 The first heater worked off a car's cooling system was produced, in the US.
1935 The first 'unitary' construction car (with chassis and body combined) was produced, by Opel in Germany.
1935 The prototype of the Volkswagen Beetle was built, but production did not begin until 1945. Over 20 million have been produced to date.
1936 The first production diesel engined car, the Mercedes-Benz 206D, was introduced, in Germany.
1938 The Nash Motor Co of Wisconsin, USA, introduced airconditioning.
1949 Chrysler introduced disc brakes on all four wheels.
1951 Chrysler introduced power-assisted steering.
1953 The first successful radial-ply tyre, the Michelin 'X', entered production in France.
1959 The Austin Mini was launched. It became the first British car to exceed the million mark, and over five million have been produced to date.
1963 The first rotary engine (Wankel) was introduced in a production car, the NSU Spyder, in Germany.
1967 General Motors produced their 100 millionth car.
1970 Robots were first used on production lines, by Nissan of Japan, at Oppana.
The 1980s have brought many developments, such as the general introduction of turbo-charged engines, anti-lock brakes and four-wheel-drive on standard production cars.

Glossary

Acrylic A chemically based paint which is baked on to surfaces at high temperatures. Its characteristics are long term durability, freedom from fade, good gloss retention and resistance to chipping. It is used by most motor manufacturers.

AGV Automatic Guided Vehicle, a battery-powered tug directed by means of a cable embedded in the factory floor and which creates a magnetic field to guide it and its trailers of components to the work station.

Assembly track A moving conveyor on which the car is built.

Automation Production of cars by automatic processes with the minimum of manual work.

Body framing Assembly of understructure, side panels, roof, bulkhead and parcel shelf in a jig for welding into one complete unit.

Body in white The assembled body shell, before engine, transmission, wheels, trim and equipment are fitted.

CAD/CAM/CAE Computer Aided Design (CAD) is the use of the computer to design the car from the styling concept. Computer Aided Manufacture (CAM) is the rôle of the computer in controlling the manufacturing processes involved in car construction. Computer Aided Engineering (CAE) employs the computer to speed model development and produce the highest possible quality by testing designs before manufacture.

Carry-over The use of components of an existing model for a new car.

Cell The passenger compartment of a car, which forms a strong box to contain and protect the occupants in an accident.

Coupé A two-door hard top sports car, usually sloping to the tail and seating two persons with two occasional seats.

Demineralized water Pure H_2O, or water with salts and other chemical impurities removed. It is used for washing car bodies, as it does not cause rust.

Direct glazing Windscreens bonded to the body shell, instead of being fixed with rubber sections.

Electrostatic painting A system which uses an electrical field. The item to be painted is connected to a power source, and another connection is made to the spray gun. The sprayed paint completes the circuit and is drawn on to the item to be painted, coating it evenly.

Estate A dual-purpose car body. The rear roofline is extended to provide a spacious compartment in which the rear passenger seats can be folded down to provide extra space for luggage or equipment. Also known as a station wagon, shooting-brake, utility or ranch wagon.

Fascia The area of the car in front of the driver and below the windscreen. It houses the instruments and switches, radio, heater controls and glovebox.

Flammability A material which has high flammability, such as rubber-based adhesive, is one which could easily catch fire.

Floorpan The base of a car body. With integral bodies, which have no chassis as such, the floorpan is the bottom of the rigid box which forms the bodyshell.

Hatchback Body style usually associated with small and medium-size cars in which the rear end opens up completely as on an estate, to give access for luggage. The rear seats fold as on an estate, though as the back end slopes more, the capacity is not as great.

Hopper A container or large bin used for carrying away waste materials from the production line.

Industrial laser Controlled light beam used for accurate measurement of body dimensions during assembly.

Internal combustion engine An engine in which the power is generated internally by a mixture of fuel and air. In a diesel this is ignited through heat caused by compression. In a petrol (gas) engine, the mixture is exploded by a spark.

Jig An accurate frame to hold components in position during assembly.

KanBan A Japanese word meaning 'just in time', used to describe the system of continuously supplying components to the assembler without the need to hold large stocks.

Lost wax A process used in casting. Hard wax is used for making a pattern from an original so that copies can be produced. The process is used by Rolls-Royce in the production of the 'Spirit of Ecstasy' radiator mascot.

Mainframe Master computer from which others operate.

Numerical co-ordinates Measurements on a vehicle or component which are recorded and stored in the computer.

Oven Enclosed area where the freshly painted body is baked at high temperatures to harden it off.

Pillars Uprights on a body, which frame the doors and windows. The front pillar on either side of the windscreen is the 'A' pillar; that in the centre between front and rear doors is the 'B' pillar.

Plant Another name for the factory.

Pneumatic tyre Standard vehicle tyre, made up of a rubber compound on a metal or fabric casing, and filled with air to maintain its shape and act as a cushion against road shocks.

Press shop Section of factory where body panels are pressed from sheet steel.

Pretreatment Preparation of body shell before painting. This includes cleaning, phosphating and electrocoating to protect the metal from corrosion and to provide a base for the paint.

Production car A car built in a series. The opposite is the prototype, or one-off.

Radiator shell In modern mass production cars the radiator is enclosed beneath the bonnet and behind a grille. Rolls-Royce still follows the old style, in which the radiator is mounted within a distinctive casing, or radiator shell.

R & D Research and Development, the constant search for and evaluation of new materials, products and processes.

Robotization The use of robots to carry out particular assembly operations.

Rolling road Test facility for checking suspension, wheel alignment, steering, engine power, braking and exhaust emission on completed car.

Saloon Conventional car body style, also known as a sedan, with front and rear seats, two or four side doors, and the luggage carried in a separate rear compartment (boot, or trunk.)

Sensors Electrical terminals set at particular points of an engine or on a component to relay to the instrument panel that the part is working correctly. For example, a sensor in a disc brake pad will switch on a warning light when the pad becomes too worn to be safe.

Sign-off The final passing of a completed car after checking and testing, ready for despatch to the dealer.

Sills Outer edge of the floorpan which forms a rigid side rail beneath the doors.

Skin The external panelling of the car.

Spoiler An air deflector on the front or rear of a car designed to increase the aerodynamic efficiency of the body.

Sub-assembly Separate production of units such as doors, ready for feeding to the main assembly line.

Suspension The part of the car between wheels and body which locates the road wheels and acts to cushion the body and its occupants against road shock. It is also the major item in determining the way in which the car handles. The suspension is generally built up of steel coil or leaf springs and tubular shock absorbers aided by steel tie rods and pivoted arms. Air or liquid are also used on some cars – for example air on the Citroën and liquid on certain versions of the Austin Mini.

Test cell Enclosed building with soundproof chamber for testing an engine running at speed.

Three-box Term for standard saloon shape. The 'boxes' are the engine compartment, passenger space and rear boot.

Tooling Equipping the assembly area with robots, welding and other machinery for production. General tooling is applicable to several models whereas specific tooling relates to one particular model of car.

Transmission Gearbox and drive shafts carrying the engine's power to the road wheels. Also known as a driveline.

Transponder Electronic device mounted in a can-shaped casing and hung beneath cars during assembly. The electronics are programmed with information on the car under construction – such as engine and transmission, power steering, individual model, etc. Used by General Motors in Britain and by Austin Rover. Coming into use with other manufacturers.

Trim Soft furnishings and interior items of a car, including carpets, upholstery, polished wood panels, and door cappings.

Underfloor, Underbody, Underframe see **Understructure.**

Understructure Floorpan pressing and sub-assemblies of car body.

VDU Visual Display Unit. Television-type screen displaying information in visual form on a computer.

Work station Point in manufacture on an assembly track or line where an operation is carried out.

Saloon

Hatchback

Estate

Coupé

Index

Acknowledgements

Threshold Books and the publishers gratefully acknowledge the help given by Ford Motor Co. Ltd. and Vauxhall Motors Ltd.

Illustration credits
Photographs: Action Plus Photographic page 3 (top); Aston Martin Lagonda Ltd. 28 (top); Austin Rover Group 12 (left), 16 (top, bottom), 17 (centre, bottom), 19 (centre), 23 (bottom left), 26 (left), 27 (bottom left); Avon Tyres Ltd 20 (bottom); Barnaby's Picture Library 2; Camera Press 3 (centre); Coleman Milne 29 (top, bottom); Daimler-Benz AG 8 (top), 22, 27 (top); Ford Motor Co. Ltd. 4/5, 6 (top, centre, bottom), 7 (top, bottom), 9 (top, centre), 12 (right), 13 (top), 14 left, 17 (top), 18 (top, centre), 20 (top, centre), 21 (top), 23 (top left), 24 (top), 25 (top, bottom), 26 (right), 27 (bottom right); Lancia 3 (bottom), 18/19; Nissan Motor Co. Ltd. 8 (bottom), 9 (bottom), 23 (top right); Rolls-Royce Motors Ltd. 28 (centre); Vauxhall Motors Ltd. 10/11, 13 (bottom), 15, 19 (top), 21 (bottom), 23 (bottom right), 24 (bottom).

Diagrams and drawings: Ray Burrows 8 (top), 13 (bottom), 14, 27 (bottom left), 28 (bottom), 31; Mel Nichols Ltd. 10/11.

Picture research: Pat Mandel.

First published in 1987
by Faber and Faber Limited,
3 Queen Square, London WC1N 3AU

Typeset by August Filmsetting, Haydock, St. Helens

Printed and bound in Italy by New Interlitho, Milan
All rights reserved

© Threshold Books Limited, 1987

The How It Is Made series was conceived, designed, and produced
by Threshold Books Limited,
661 Fulham Road, London SW6 5PZ

General Editor: Barbara Cooper

British Library Cataloguing in Publication Data 629.2

Taylor, John
  Motor cars.—(How it is made)
  1. Automobile industry and trade
  Juvenile literature
  I. Title   II. Series
  629.2'34   TL278
  ISBN 0–571–14729–1